For anyone who's ever grown up,
for anyone who's ever had to grow up;

and for Fofo and for Monteha and
for all my sisters and for my brothers,

and for my mother three times
and then my father.

i wish
this skin
had come
with instructions

—emi mahmoud

sisters' entrance

Emtithal Mahmoud

Andrews McMeel
PUBLISHING®

contents

The Girl with Ribbons in Her Hair   1

Sometimes God Answers   21

The Life of a Refugee Is Counted in Moments   43

Stand Up to Allah   67

We Never Hire Gravediggers   89

Index   119

the girl with
ribbons in her hair

People Like Us

Memories of my childhood live
between the rings of sand around my ankles
and the desert heat in my lungs.

I still believe that nothing washes
worry from tired skin better than the Nile
and my grandma's hands.

Every day I go to school
with the weight of dead neighbors
on my shoulders.

The first time I saw bomb smoke,
it didn't wind and billow like the heat
from our kitchen hearth.

It forced itself on the Darfur sky,
smothering the sun
with tears that it stole
from our bodies.

The worst thing about genocide
isn't the murder, the politics, the hunger,
the government-paid soldiers

that chase you across borders
and into camps.

It's the silence.

For three months, they closed the schools down
because people like us are an eyesore.

The first month, we took it.
The second, we waited.

The third month, we met underneath the date palm
   trees,
drinking up every second our teachers gave us,
turning fruit pits into fractions.
On the last day, they came with a message
Put them in their place.

We didn't stand a chance.
Flesh was never meant to dance
with silver bullets.

So we prayed for the sun to come
and melt daggers from our backs.

Lifted our voices up to God
until the clouds were spent for weeping
and the sand beneath our toes
echoed with the song of every soul
that ever walked before us.

I hid underneath the bed that day
with four other people.

Twelve years later and I can't help but wonder
where my cousins hid when the soldiers
torched the houses,
threw the bodies
in the wells.

If the weapons didn't get you,
the poison would.

Sometimes, they didn't want to use bullets
because it would cost them more than we did.
I've seen sixteen ways to stop a heart.

When you build nations on someone's bones
what sense does it make to break them?

In one day, my mother choked on rifle smoke,
my father washed the blood from his face,
my uncles carried half the bodies
to the hospital,
the rest to the grave.

We watched.
For every funeral we planned
there were sixty we couldn't.

Half the sand in the Sahara
tastes a lot like powdered bone.

When the soldiers came,
our blood on their ankles,
I remember their laces,
scarlet footprints on the floor.

I remember waking to the sound
of hushed voices in the night
etched with the kind of sorrow
that turns even the loudest dreams
to ash.

Our parents came home with broken collarbones
and the taste of fear carved
into their skin.

It was impossible to believe in anything.

Fear is the coldest thing in the desert,
and it burns you—
bows you down to half your height
and owns you.

And no one hears you,
because what could grow
in the desert
anyway?

August

Remorse is my grandmother's pear tree,
me bent over a tin pail washing dishes
in the sun of our final moments.

The water drawn from a drying well
by a niece I did not know.

The porcelain scraping sand
against the pail, eroding
like my family.

Like the strained conversation
between my mother sitting across
from the woman she hadn't seen
in five years—

Me, the daughter she hadn't seen in one.

Sisters' Entrance

Ms. Amal tried to teach us about love
in Sunday school.

She said:

God is a poet.
He opened up the sky,
spilled His word across our skin,
and called it revelation.

This aging giant, with
a soft spot for affection, made
you and me and a soul mate for every one of us
as long as we wait.

We couldn't.

Restless hands clasped under classroom tables.
Obsidian eyes locked across prayer aisles

as we slowly opened our minds to
the gravity of one another.

Passion is a paradox in the house of God;
a weightless anchoring that draws you
closer to your Creator and
makes you fear the heart he gave you.

You confuse enchantment with doubt,
desire with insubordination,
stranger to the weight of it all.

That's when they started separating us:

girls' side, boys' side
and then by age,
they introduced us to the Sisters' Entrance.

Sesame Candy

Remember the summer we planted arugula
in the sidewalk garden

the same year the boys covered their heads in ash
the same year we didn't know anyone new
the same year grandpa called all of us wicked?

I go back there sometimes, next to the dogwood tree
and see the place where our garden used to grow
the magnolia, the figs

I take the seeds home with me
I keep them in a desk drawer
waiting for a drier year,

or a rainy one, or a reason
I keep hoping that I'll turn away
and look back and see those girls playing again,
the ones we used to be before the war.

Afternoon Naps in the House of God

I lay my head on cushions

so clean

they smell like piety,

back propped against a wall

so firm

it sticks out
     like doubt.

Loose Threads

Our teacher's cousin planned
her wedding for the week after Ramadan.

We filled the hall with decorations,
sequins spilling from the closet
in the corner.

Our veils unfurled.
Hooded sisters opening their pages
to one another.

A quick break to pray Maghreb
a whole room full of laughs.

Our belly dance shoes at the door
lest the rugs start to bruise
from our footsteps.

Shoulder to shoulder,
wrist to wrist,
we bore all.

That's the secret to the sisters' side:
no drama, no apologies
no worries, no reservations,
no sleeves.

Euphoria at Community Prayer

Belief is not transferable,
but, not unlike guilt, it burns brightly
by association.

#MuslimParents

Layla and Ahmed had
their first kiss in
the basement of the mosque
where we keep the
extra prayer rugs.

The Imam caught them—
tricked them into thinking
they were married.

Layla's parents laughed
all the way home,
said, *Relax, you're seven.*

Ahmed's parents
took away his iPhone.

The Imam on Charity

I counted three Maseratis,

two Ferraris, and

a Lamborghini

in the parking lot.

Reach into your pockets

and

cough up some piety.

One-Drop Well

The girl with ribbons in her hair has
ribbons on the inside of her wrist
I saw her losing hope today.

They say if you hold love in your heart
And not in your hand
You'll be free to break the fall

I tell her, I don't fall
I dive

Headfirst
Into a patchwork pavement
The gravel in my teeth a testament
That these parts of me were salvaged
from a story much older than myself—

from the first small boy
who grew up to be
my father's father,
from the first young girl
who didn't give in to the wish
to rest completely

from my grandfather
who didn't give up the mountain
from the aunt who raised her sister's children
when my grandmother couldn't

from the tears that fell
when they broke the rock
to dig the well

the water's song
the bedrock's gift
the one-man road my father dug

At a funeral, my great-aunt grabs my arm.
I don't know her. It hurts her more than the son
    who died—
My uncle, Ocean—his sister says
the sea has dried for her.

I broke myself 500 times
before the pieces started making sense.

From the bloodied mayhem
I make new
me, who I want to be, who I am.

Three sisters who contradict each other
and yet don't exist without
the other.

I dig again
to reclaim the things lay buried there
the hopes I shed after every tumble
the elbow I grazed when I was three

the boy I don't love anymore
the family I still do.

sometimes God answers

The Talk

I asked my mother
where babies come from.
She said:

"When two parents want
a baby
they do . . . a

special prayer.

If God wants them to
have a baby,

they do.

If not,

they do the prayer again
and again
and again.

Sometimes God answers.
Sometimes He doesn't."

Sustenance

The word of God
ringing above
competes with
dinner plans and
neighborly
gossip.

The
Holy Spirit
sounds
so
human
in this room.

Year-Round

Babies cry
on the women's side,

fists firm, eyes shut, bodies screaming.

Frail voices
extend the reach of one another.

Disrupt the call to prayer.

We take them to their fathers.

Babies cry on the men's side too.

The Bride

I met her on her wedding day,
walked up to her, and smiled.

No one ever talks to the bride.
I thought it might be interesting
to try something new.
Break tradition.

Henna patterns wrapped
around her wrists, climbed
up her arms,
spreading blossoms on tender flesh.

Her lips were a wilted crimson,
tilted ever so slightly to the side.
The perfect almost smile.

The first thing her mother taught her
was to wipe the tears
before the blood dries.

Shredded knees heal, but shame
never fades away. Don't climb trees
or ride bikes, that's how little girls
lose their virginity.

She sat on a porcelain throne,
beads and bows holding
plastic flowers to the armrests.
are you alright? I asked
  I shouldn't cry she said,
fingers catching tired tears.
it's fine to cry, you'll be happy later.
  I shouldn't cry
how long have you known him?
  I don't.

She was 17 years old,
just graduated high school.
Her parents sent her to college
because an educated girl
can earn a bigger dowry,

but this mister didn't mind a country girl.
He grew up with her father.
Didn't need an intellectual,
just someone who could feed the kids
while he raised them.

She was a mail-order bride
and her father licked the stamp.
I cried.

How many weddings have I been to?

She just got off the plane

twelve hours ago, and they already
started dressing her.
No time to take measurements
so they pinned satin to her skin,
tucked her in to the time-tested wire frame
our ancestors welded.

If you put a girl in a steel corset
you'll never have to hear her scream.
She was gorgeous.

You could put anyone in her dress
and it wouldn't make a difference.
We were guests of the groom
this was his wedding.

No one knew her name.
She only spoke Arabic.
No one knew her name.
And she danced until the tears came.

The middle-aged used-to-be brides
explained it away.
She remembered her mother
       they said.
Brides always cry when they remember
their mothers.

She'll have her fifth child by thirty.

My parents protected me
from all the broken men
and their flesh-eating fingers.
Said one day I'd find someone who
can cook as well as my dad
and is almost as smart as my mom,
who'd hold me so close that I could
breathe in their memories.

When I told my parents about the bride
and all we could do was hold her hand,
it killed me.

Tonight he'll crush the henna blossoms
on her wrists with the same hands the man
next door threw at his wife last Thursday,
the same fists that taught a daughter
to keep her mouth shut.

He'll flatten the ridges of her spine
and she'll hold her tongue.
Bite the screams as they come.
Wipe the tears before the blood dries.
No one ever talks to the bride.

The Things She Told Me

I asked my mother to lend me her strength.
She proceeded to lift an entire planet
from her back.

A pearl necklace, her wedding dress,
rubber gloves from the kitchen sink,

the shoes she wore in elementary school,
her diploma, two fistfuls of hope

and a tattered legacy of fear,
the kiss from the boy next door,
her father's walking stick,
two pence for the market,

a basket full of the finest okra,
an envelope of desert sand,
three safety pins,
one pair of sturdy khaki pants—
good for work but not for raising children—
and one pen.

She said, with a shaking voice,
Learn these things, before they teach you.

Death loves a woman, but we are still here.

And the moon is crying, or maybe singing
and the stars look down in mourning
as we melt hatred and weave compassion,
gather the waste from each body
and weld resilience.

We do this every day—make a good thing
out of nothing,
be the strong ones,
be okay even when we're not.

But today, we're more than okay,
we are women.
So, take my strength, I've got plenty.

Take my hands, I've got two.
Take my voice, let it guide you
and if it shakes, ask yourself:

when the earth shakes,
do you think that she's afraid?

Jezebel

A praying mantis
Savors each dismantled mate.
Love or gluttony?

Why I Haven't Told You Yet

To the guy I like: *wake the fuck up.*
I'm standing here, all morning dew brilliant
and you, brick wall, bane of my existence,
with the gaping mouth and the misdirected
    conviction.

I want to cry for you,
but I don't because this, this is hilarious.
This is the cruelest kind of mirth—
To be standing 3 inches from the center of your
    affection
and yet still, there's a universe,
a river of obstinacy
a field of missed opportunities and horrible, horrible
    timing standing between us.

You stupid, stupid manchild.
With the barely there smile
and the dimple on your right cheek,
I left the girl in me standing at an altar of her own
    fears waiting for you,
but you're here
at the receiving end of this poem.

A friend once told me that romance is like a house;
you, the girl, open the window, and he, the boy,
    climbs in.

Hey, asshole! The window is open!

That's when I start wondering why I'm standing in a
  house.
A house built by a generation of men and women
  who have a habit of putting people in pretty boxes.

I wonder what broken architect laid these bricks.
Is this how it's going to be?
Me, walking the corridors of my own mind,
seeing the telltale signs of a boy who doesn't belong
  there?
His handprint on the mirror,
his silhouette at the corner table.
I open my eyes
You once said I'm cute when I'm angry,
Well, I'm about to look phenomenal.

We teach our girls to quarantine their emotions—
isolate heart and reason or risk perceptions of
  hysteria.
We're taught that our anger is a misconception,
that our discontent will pass as long as we smile
  pretty,
clean up nice, and play into this courtship dichotomy.
This twisted game of act and receive
where your role is assigned at birth.
Well, this is me telling you

that the only winning move is not to play.
So, I'm gonna burn this whole house down.

I'm ripping through these walls
so fast that millennia of cages will rattle loose
and every person who's ever stood at this window
And every other person who's ever stood on the
    other side, too paralyzed to move, will walk free.
This is an official notice—

Emi has left the building.
But first, a word of advice: for those of you still
    dancing around houses—*just use the door.*

Prospects

The new kid named Adil
came to our mosque.

At 12, he
checked all the right
boxes:

Great at soccer,
straight As,
pious,
good to his mother.

The girls fawned
over this ideal
we had come to strive for.

One day,
we asked which of us he would
choose.

He said he's going
to grow up
and marry Beyoncé.

Telephone

Passing blessings

Hand to hand

A game of

Spiritual

Telephone

Until the message is transformed in each heart
Everyone smiles at a different truth

How to Translate a Joke

A man walks into the market looking for a date.
He asks the village playboy for help.
The village playboy says,
watch, and learn.

He walks up to a girl selling honey
and says, *do you have any honey, honey?*
She swoons, gives him honey
and a kiss.

He walks up to a woman selling flowers,
Do you have any flowers, you rose?
She melts, gives him flowers
and a kiss.

He walks to a third woman,
Do you have any sugar, sugar?

She practically dies,

gives him sugar,
and kisses him twice.

The playboy comes back,
your turn, stud.
The man apprehensively walks up
to a woman selling dairy
and says,

Do you have any milk, cow?

Realize that humor transcends
all boundaries; that laughter
is a language that knows no borders;

that this joke I heard in Arabic
makes perfect sense in English,
and French, and any other dialect—

Realize that we call women cows
in every language.
Realize that humor leaves little room
for questions, and even less room
for victims and even less room
for apologies.

Realize that in one version of this joke,
the man is looking to pick up girls,
in another, he's looking for a wife,
in a third, he's looking
for an answer.

And maybe the cow slaps him,
or the cow asks him to leave
and he tries again,
or she walks faster,
clutches her purse
or maybe she threatens him
and is jailed for treason or maybe

the cow sues him
and the case is dismissed
or they settle

down

We are willing to say offensive
more than we say dangerous
as if harm isn't transitive
as if it isn't something you do
to another person.

We like to pretend that I am not
as uncomfortable alone
on the streets of New York
as I am on the streets of Nepal,
that a stroll in Philly or Indiana,
Minnesota, doesn't bring as many stares
as in India, or Sudan, or Egypt

That violence is a *third world* problem,
that it isn't here, hiding
in a conversation, or a bouquet,
or a market
that not being alone makes a difference.

If they don't get the joke, say it again,
smile more this time, repeat the punch line,
pause for dramatic effect
use jazz hands. If you have to,

laugh.

In another version, that man walks
into the market, looking for a date,
and leaves with an unwilling woman,
a bounty.

In my language, I am a sweet,
and if not that, a decoration,
a flower, a gift.

He walks up to the girl selling honey,
she gives him her eyes,
her arms, her silence.

He walks up to the girl selling sugar,
she practically dies.

Sometimes God Answers

He walks up to the girl selling flowers,
calls her a rose, strips all her thorns
sticks her in a bouquet,
she fights, he breaks her,
calls her a dead thing,
she melts, is trampled
in the market.

There are four women in the joke,
none of them speak.

Realize that humor transcends
all boundaries; that laughter
is a language that knows no borders;
that this joke I heard in Arabic

hurts just as much in English,
and French, and any other dialect—
In the last version, the man is foaming
at the mouth with another girl's jugular
around his teeth, his Adam's apple
making excuses for him
from all the way
over there.

And the market is cheering,
the girl's hair a bracelet around his wrist
and the market is still cheering,
or the audience, or the schoolyard,
or the other men
and he asks her name.
She says,

You left a box of your things
in my stomach.
Are you still trying to find
yourself on another girl's
neck?

Last week, my seven-year-old brother
said that I am the reason he wakes up
every morning.

I gave him a hug, he whispered to my mother,
works every time—
I saw the fear in her eyes.
We laughed.

the life of a refugee is
counted in moments

Cinderblock

A brick broke through
the window of our masjid today.
The Imam unlocks the doors every morning,
sweeps up the glass,
replaces the window
before afternoon prayer.

No fear in sacred spaces.

The brick still sits in the main office;
a gentle reminder of the hand
that broke through our sanctuary.
The world is vast inside the masjid
but small everywhere else.

No Funeral

Elder Shama collapsed after
Sisters' Quran circle—
Cardiac arrest—

The other women—
crying—

gathered their children,
started screaming,
started praying.

My mother—
silent—
started CPR.

I—
used to this—
called the police.

September

My grandmother's eyes courting cataracts
hands held firm by the arthritis
her favorite braids dangling with the fabric
she still wore on summer days

You're my mother and you're going to die here
my mother's body to my grandmother
This house needs me in it
my grandmother to the air.

the women in my family are places
apart. To remember them is to remember
what we
have left.

She Threw Things out of Windows and I Watched

We learned to hit the ground together
when the bullets came.

My sister and I used to spend our afternoons
tethered to the windows
along the far side of our apartment,
watching the days pass as we aged.

Time moved breathtakingly slowly
back then; as if someone had dipped
our entire childhood in glue
and set the mismatched pieces out to dry.

As soon as she could walk,
Fofo became obsessed with flying
So, she threw things out of windows
and I watched.

First the house keys, my mother's dress,
a series of everyday items

every spoon or doll or book
met a swift and thorough end.

That's when the banging came.

Quick successive bursts, a choir
of bleeding mouths, a series of screams
Both inside and outside of our apartment.

I couldn't stop looking at my mother,
face pressed to the ground,
arms pinning both my sister and me to her sides

We stayed there until the sun began to set,
Playing dead in a high-rise in Yemen.

Years later, in Philly, we laughed and sang,
the worst behind us,
aunties and uncles feasting at our table
an orphans' communion,
a group of Sudanese people far enough
to forget the war

When the banging came, everybody hit the floor,
from the three-year-olds by the stairs
to the uncles in the dining room,

My face hit the carpet,
our bodies remember
what our senses forget.

To a family of immigrants,
the Fourth of July sounds
like a firing squad,
like the debt collector,
like the dictator coming to call.

It sounds like sunset for the last time or
it sounds like faces hitting the concrete
their voices still remaining, still pleading,
still praying in the wrong language.

Classrooms

The first time I was asked to leave a classroom
the teacher said I was too smart
That the other kids needed to catch up

For generations, the women in my family
have been denied a seat in the classroom
and there I stood, repeating the cycle
for a completely different reason

I wonder if the teacher knew the bite of hunger
that drove me to her doorstep,
If she'd tasted sorrow's whip
that sewed the silence on my tongue

Did she know that this language
tasted like sandpaper the first time?
That I used to write on beaten earth
and cement walls?
That once I held a pen, I never
wanted to put it down?

Did she know the difference she made
that day?
The danger she carved back
into my safe space

All my life, I've been staring
at painted ceilings.
Standing on the shoulders of giants
that will never claim me.
Learning history as if it hadn't tried
to erase me, as if I hadn't spent afternoons
in the hallways because my teacher didn't know
what to do with a girl who knew too much.

She told me to lighten up, turn that frown
upside down like a pretty girl.

The second time I left the classroom
was to see a doctor because of a burn.
Hot tea on my arm, my mother's tears, and an
    afternoon that changed me.
The doctor said, *such a shame, what a scar on such a*
    beautiful girl

The third time was to head to the Capitol Building
on an April afternoon and sit among men

I've been hanging on to these moments
Learning to keep things inside,
You wear a mask long enough
and it starts to feel like home.

If I could go back, I wouldn't have left that classroom,
I would've stood, reciting arithmetic
like I hadn't lost anything

Like I haven't seen the world end
a thousand times.
Like I hadn't held my mother as she cried
or my father as he broke over and over again.

Like I never played hopscotch in a war zone
Like I haven't woken up
on the wrong side of heaven
every day since.

Where I come from, the opposite of learning
is death. The price of speaking is flesh.
The weight of being a woman scars
deeper than the most unforgiving of wounds

But not today, not among my sisters,
not in this room, not in the next,
Not in a world where I can stand,
me here woman, proud

speaking like the world didn't try to erase me.
wearing my wings and vaulting
fists raised toward the sky

When your existence is an act of defiance, live.

Boy in the Sand

I saw a boy make his final stand today,
face buried in a sea of sand, body prone, bent, broken
like the waves.

His chest was not moving,
his heart did not beat, everything around him was
    suspended
in the varied turmoil of land and water;
push and pull—as if each were trying to reclaim him.

It is like that sometimes
when I see the corpse of a stranger. That kind of
    death,
from the outside of someone else's final breath . . .
it makes the air stop,
the ocean turn more slowly,
the earth a cradle
a cemetery
a monument
a stone
like a dead boy resting in the sand.

Head over Heels

They hand me the microphone as my shoulder sinks
   under the weight of this dress;
The woman says,
The one-millionth refugee just left South Sudan; can
   you comment?

I feel my feet rock back and forth
on the heels my mother bought
Begging the question,

do we stay, or is it safer to choose flight?

My mind echoes through the numbers:
One million gone, 400,000 dead in Darfur,
two million displaced
and this lump takes over my throat as if each of
   those bodies found a grave right here in my
   esophagus.

Our once country—
all west, and south, and east, and north—
so restless, the Nile couldn't hold us together
and you ask me to summarize?

They talk about the numbers as if this isn't still
   happening,
As if 500,000 didn't just die in Syria,
as if 3,000 aren't still making their final stand
at the bottom of the Mediterranean,
as if there aren't entire volumes full of factsheets about
   our genocide and now you want me to write one?

Fact: we never talked over breakfast because the
warplanes would swallow our voices.

Fact: my grandfather didn't want to leave home
so he died in a war zone.

Fact: a burning bush without God is just a fire.

I measure the distance between what I know and
   what is safe to say on a microphone.
Do I talk about sorrow, displacement?
Do I mention the violence?
How it's never as simple as what we see on TV?
How there are weeks' worth of fear before the
   camera is on?

Do I talk about our bodies? How they are 60 percent
    water, but we still burn like driftwood?
Do I tell her the men died first? Mothers forced to
    watch the slaughter?
That they came for our children?
Scattering them across the continent
until our homes sank, that even castles sink at the
    bite of the bomb?

Do I mention the elderly? Our heroes—
too weak to run too expensive to shoot?
How they would march them hands raised, rifles at
    their backs into the fire?
How their walking sticks kept the flames alive?

It sounds too harsh for a bundle of wires and an
    audience to swallow; too relentless,
like the valley that filled with the putrid smoke of
    our deaths.
Is it better in verse? Can a stanza become a burial
    shroud?

Will it sting less if I say it softly?
Will the pain leave when the microphone does?
If you don't see me cry, will you listen better?
30 seconds for the sound bite and now 3 minutes
    for the poem. Why does every word feel like I'm
    saying my last?

My tongue goes dry, the same way we died—
becoming ash without ever having been coal.
I feel my left leg go numb and realize that I locked
    my knees,
bracing for impact.

I never wear shoes I can't run in.

Dr. Poem

His daughter was dying, so he begged my father
to look after her.
My dad said, *don't worry, bones heal;*
    it's the waiting that gets you.
In that moment, I was convinced
that my father could fix everything.

I am not my father.
I stare at my hands each day
wondering when they'll look like his.
It was midday and the doctors
were stressed but still moving.

I was working in the only birthing hospital
for miles in my homeland, Darfur.
When I go home, they call it
community service—
the prodigal daughter returns
from America to heal her people
with the things she learned in her ivory tower—

but there are things in medicine
we don't have scientific names for.
I was one of six doctors, I am not a doctor.

When they brought in our patients
with all that blood on the outside
of their bodies
and tears,
and dust,
and the mothers wondering
if they can resurrect the earth
to plead with the angels of death
on their behalf,

The operation room became a trial
the scalpel a gavel
and every doctor a perjurer
on this broken witness stand.

We were arbiters of death.
This isn't how it was meant to be.
When my cousin's stomach split open
and the confetti of his gut littered the floor;
When my uncle drank the river through his lungs;
When the illness stole the girl
across the street in broad daylight;
When my brother caved to the embrace
of the second bullet;

When the cancer came for all the things
the war had left behind—
I wished I were my father or someone,
or God—a doctor a doctor a doctor—
But what do you say when their first question
is about the war?

What happens when they hate you
for bringing them back?
Or when the insurance won't pay for the operation
and you still can't afford it either?

Or when they bomb the hospital
so you have to operate without borders?
Or when they hold you at gunpoint
for transporting vaccinations so the children
can survive until after the war?
I still don't know what comes
after the war.

Or when the husband won't sign the consent form
for his wife's treatment
because a fully conscious woman
doesn't have that right in my homeland.

When I tell you misogyny is life-threatening,
When I tell you the patriarchy can kill you,
this is what I mean.
In one day, we had six emergency
C-sections.

An entire would-be classroom of infants
passed through our halls,
each of them fighting for their lives
without any knowledge
of how many of us had to fight for it first.

I'm ashamed to admit the guilt
of being a doctor in the war zone,
Bringing children into Armageddon.
But, they have to understand that their lives matter
and I can't fix anything, but I can make them
   breathe,   *breathe,*
                    breathe.

Bird-Watching on Lesvos Island

I met a woman, her mother, and her son
all under the subtle shade of a tent—
three generations held together
in one morsel of time.

The life of a refugee is counted in moments.
In this moment, we were bird-watching
on Lesvos Island.

The sun melted the clouds across our vision
as the first bird spiraled brilliantly
toward the Aegean shore.

To go from bird-watching to boat-watching
in Greece is to witness the world unfurl.

I was told of days when the birds came in hoards
broken-winged and heaving, spilling forth 50 to 80
    hatchlings at a time,

each broken shell another person seeking rest.
floating rubber albatrosses, box-figured crows,
hugged the horizon in the bitter cold.

When an island becomes a door,
who will answer?

If enough eyes see a body in the water
and no hands reach out to rescue her,
did she really die?

This time, when the world left infants
to take their first steps at the edge

of humanity;

when the seams broke and the threads
lay society bare;
the eyes came and the helping hands
followed.

Imagine rivers full of people carrying people
on their backs.
Imagine shores covered in footprints,
and wheelchair tracks,

the passion it takes to swallow the wind,
kiss the October Sea
and meet the boats.

I've seen how paperwork can divide families,
separating mother and father
with the stroke of a pen.
How firm handshakes can unravel entire nations
when the stage is big enough.

If I had the power, I would have paper-mached
those contracts;
I would have lined the ceilings
with paper cup lights;
I would have painted every wall cerulean
so even the smallest of palms
could reach for the sky.

I would have lined entire rooms with books
and kitchens with the warmest pies.
I would have carpeted camps with chalk
to build a home
to make a refuge, to bring the dignity back
into a concrete oasis.

I would have built a camp
that is a call to prayer
where a person who is carried in
can leave walking.

This is what I saw on Lesvos Island.
When a child is born in the context of war,
this is how you unravel the world to them
how you unveil music to their ears.

I have stood on both sides now
and I can tell you that in Lesvos,
the cats are white with brown spots
because a child's painting told me so.

That life-jacket bags are in style
because a boy named Suhaib showed me so.
That a village can all stand together
because a woman willed it so.

Safe passage begins by asking the questions
no one will dare to utter,
and becoming the answer
no one could possibly
imagine.

stand up to Allah

Take Notes

A woman came to campus.
She told us to stand up to Allah.
My friend said we do;
five times a day.

Prayer is a dialogue in
which all persons have equal access
to the microphone.

To Envy a Scavenger

Twin-size sheet, white—
burial shroud
fastened to a child.

Her mother's face carried
more death than the coffin.

Her father, for the first time in months,
the only doctor by her side

The Imam's voice hummed the scripture.

To my left,
a crow surveyed the scene.

I swung my hand toward the windowsill.
Not violence.
A plea. It took flight.

Tenets

Four men stood

smoking by the mosque,

scorched tobacco

billowing

against Moroccan-style tile.

One among them paused:

Isn't smoking forbidden?

In unison:

God is forgiving

Deliverance in the Information Age

I bought an app to track prayer:
religiosity in the palm of my hand.

It came with a compass,
tenet guide, settings for school of thought

Reminders for prayer,
supplication,
good deeds—
God in a few megabytes.

No option for rejuvenation.
No new feature for forgiveness.

If I clear data, will my sins vanish?

Can this silicone chip carry my pride,
contain my envy, my anger, my sloth?

Is this want for gilded grace not greed?

Crescent moon and star emoji,
little Mecca on my screen,
will you ask the angels for me
what salvation looks like
after 2016?

You Have a Big Imagination, or 400,000 Ways to Cry

I am a sad girl, but my face makes other plans
Focusing energy on this smile
so as not to waste it on pain.

The first thing they took was my sleep,
eyes heavy but wide open
Thinking maybe I missed something,
maybe the cavalry is still coming.

They didn't come, so I bought bigger pillows.

My grandma could cure anything by talking the life
out of it and she said
I could make a thief in a silo laugh
in the middle of our raging war.

War makes a broken marriage bed out of sorrow—
you want nothing more than to disappear,
yet your heart can't bear to leave.

But love, love is the armor we carried across the
   borders of our broken homeland.
A hasty mix of stories that last long after the flavor
   is gone, and muscle memory that overcomes
even the most bitter of times.

My memory is spotted with days of laughing
until I cried or crying until I laughed—
laughter and tears are both involuntary
reactions, testaments of human expression.
So allow me to express, that if I make you laugh,
It's usually on purpose
and if I make you cry, I promise I'll still think
you are beautiful.

I learned love in France, my cousin Zeinab bedridden
on a random afternoon.

Dilated fibromyalgia—her heart muscles expanded
    until they no longer functioned

I hadn't seen her since that last time
in Sudan together and there I was at her bedside
in a 400-year-old hospital in Paris.

This is for Zeinab who wanted to hear poems.
Suddenly, English Arabic and French
were not enough. Every word I knew
was empty noise, and she said,
        well get on with it

It was the most important stage I've ever been on—
surrounded by family, by remnants of a people
who were given as a dowry
to relentless war
but still manage
to make pearls of this life.

The family that taught me not only to laugh
but to live in the face of death
Placing their hands across the sun
saying, *See that, I'll meet you there!*

and for Zeinab who on her deathbed
wanted to hear
poems.

Most days I am only sandstone, but
in her arms I felt like gold.
And we laughed and we loved, and I asked,
Isn't it strange that the only problem
is your heart was too big?

October, or My Uncle Calls to Say Grandma Has Died

The water drained my blood, my fingers ginger roots
in a bodiless house, a cathedral where no one prays,
a mosque burned to dust, a woman
out of time.

You're my mother and you're going to die here
        me to my grandmother's daughter.
How can I leave when she won't
        my mother to the silence, my mother to the soap
my mother to the pear tree, my mother to the bed.
My mother to her shoes, my mother to the sky,
my mother to the heat, my mother to the woman
she would not see until the next life.

Dad

When I was little, you built us a snow globe
with your own hands,
stretched out the glass around us
until everything was suspended.

Peace floating in the spaces between our fingers.
We lived in slow motion.
In there I was your apprentice,
handling screwdrivers and monkey wrenches
faster than I could name them.

How many times have I told you,
stainless steel is not for little girls?
I know, but it was the only way we could ever fix
  things that didn't break us.

Dad, it's the third time this month
that I'll watch you walk out our door
off to mend bridges that always lead away
from our family.

Twelve years and the bodies of my aunts,
uncles, cousins, all the branches of our family tree
haven't stopped hitting the ground
so you were enlisted to pick up the pieces.

An activist pulling peace by the skin of your teeth,
talking to humanitarians and politicians—
your words a useless currency,
their lives slipping through our fingers
Faster than the earth that swallowed them.

You insisted they depended on it.
Dad, our lives depended on you
and every time I had that thought
the guilt would force the tears back through my eyes
telling me not to be selfish.

There are things so much bigger than father-daughter.
Your dad doesn't belong to you.
I know, but Dad, why are we fighting for a country
    that never wanted us alive?

The other day, I walked into the kitchen
and you were washing the dishes.
Humanitarian, peacemaker, hero to our people
pouring soap on a little yellow sponge and washing
    away the peanut butter jelly from lunch.

Dad, you're amazing.
I hate that I couldn't tell you that while you were gone.
Twelve years I learned to live without touching you,
because people depended on you
I tried so hard not to do that—

stopped wiping the salt from my face
and accepted it: with so many people to carry
on your shoulders, I couldn't expect
you to remember what it feels like to have me there.
We couldn't have you, so I had to be you.
I learned to file taxes, talk to teachers,
take my brothers to the doctor,
cook, clean, pray just like you,
be a father's daughter in her father's shoes
and it was impossible.

I didn't know you were holding us together
with both your arms.
You've been home for months now,
so I begged you to take me with you.
I watched from a crowd of faces that look
nothing like ours,
families not nearly as frail as our own.

You argued people over politics.
I saw you cry, heard your voice
like it was my own.
You said, *I just want them to stop the killing.*
Baba,

I did not know.
You needed your father more than I ever needed mine.

Yesterday, the cupboard door fell off its hinges.
You told me to bring you the monkey wrench.
It was just like holding your hand.

Millennial

I want to be owed
something
for all this virtue, this
        righteousness—
satisfaction for sacrifice—

but that's not the usual way of things
so I join a group for young Muslims.

We hear the insides of our own
        thoughts
from the mouths of one another.

There is sorrow here and in that sorrow,
solace.

There is joy here and in that joy,
abandon.

Such arrogance it was
to have ever felt
that I was the only one
of anything.

No One Says How Easy It Is to Fall in Love, or How Hard It Is to Stay There

The one you love sits across from you at breakfast,
maybe it's your sister, or your father,
or the one who holds you closer
than any other person.

Between you is the coffee, your cell phone,
or the Atlantic Ocean
or a pillow covered in your mother's tears,
or your self-esteem again

He says *calm down* you feel the truth claw its way
out of your throat
        Pass the butter you say,
used to the part where everyone asks how you are
you say *okay* and they believe it.

Your survivor's guilt makes you apologetic
I talk a lot, sorry
        I think too fast, sorry
I count the exits in a room as quickly
as I can count the exits in a conversation,
        sorry

You try to control it, but that morning,
anxiety ties your lover to the bed and says,
     let's play.
She brings all her friends: the trembling legs,
the sweaty palms, the indoor voice,
your relationship.

You've officially been awake for only fifteen minutes
and you've already imagined every scenario
of things that could go wrong
on this day.

There are still 20 minutes left until your alarm rings,
so you imagine everything that will go wrong
tomorrow.

Then it rings. When he smiles,
the war packs her things and says
I'm leaving. The walls stop closing in,
the ceiling isn't inches from your face

and you're back in Paris, under that starless sky.
You think about kissing him,
but the Imam walks in
dangling salvation from the tip of his prayer beads

Saying things about how *God speaks softly and
carries*
a big stick, as if his sermons
weren't phallic enough already.

Then your mom brings eternal damnation into
the picture.
The temperature rises and you're not sure
if it's hell or the way his eyes look tonight.

You feel like a lie in that red dress,
heaven and hell and adolescent hormones
are picking you apart in that order.

You kiss him anyway and for a moment,
you can breathe without a ticking time bomb
on your oxygen tank.

You recognize the irony of a Muslim
with a bomb metaphor and pray to God the CIA
can't read your thoughts.

The city falls away around you.
The night air feels like a summer harvest.
The CIA, the Imam, and your mother convene in
the corner.

The bible starts looking at you funny.
You kiss him again and think this must be how the
  Red Sea feels when she tastes the Atlantic on a
  breath of wind.

But fear clamps down on your neck
so he says it first, too soon, and too quickly—
you listen anyway.

Bite down that thing you read somewhere
about how those who love first
are the first to go.

When he looks at you, forget everything,
spend the next eternity making up
for not saying it first:
carry him—the way the Nile carries Lake Victoria,
hold him, the way a traveler
hangs on to the North Star.

Love him the way the Dead Sea loves Mount Everest,
how they envelop the peaks and troughs of this
  planet,
let his best days sink into your worst,
and his worst days into your best
make home of this.

Stand Up to Allah

Every body of water, every drop,
every rain makes you think of him
and you're both from the desert
so you can't help but feel you've spent
your entire life at his mercy.

When he leaves you, it doesn't stop raining.
You're left drenched in the desert,
something you prayed for.

You start to wonder if the continents ever call for
      each other on the cold nights.
Or if Venus ever reaches for Saturn,
or if the moon ever wants to come home.

I tried to forget you, sunk all your memories
            in the river
but the waves keep tossing them back.

I want to believe that I'll see you again,
            but we don't live long where I'm from.
Venus is weeping in my arms
            The hardest part about watching you leave
is that you can.

Anxiety ties you to the bed,
            the war unpacks her things.

Islamophobia

Representation is a conversation we are seldom

invited to.

Tower Two

A night of waiting and
they didn't come for my mother's throat,
  my sister's hijab
A night of waiting and they didn't take my father's
 robes
Crush him once for his faith and once more for
     his skin
A night of waiting and the president said we were
 neighbors
And the Imam cried for the towers and our flags
      hung high over our doorsteps
And our families did not fear for our lives
And 300 girls did not disappear
And no one went to war
And the teachers didn't treat me different
And the students didn't keep their distance
   And the man on the corner did not ask me if I
   were a Christian
And the refugees did not cover the shore
And hundreds of thousands did not leave their homes
And Darfur did not go unspoken
And Syria did not go unnoticed
And the Congo, Ukraine, Egypt, Somalia
   And young mothers were not detained
And the beaches did not fill with lifeboats
And the oceans did not fill with bodies
And the bombs and the people and the children,
    the children,
      the children

And my brother was not called a nigger
And my brother was not called a sand nigger
And a college boy did not reach under my sister's scarf
  to pull her hair
And no one threw a pig's head at the mosque
                          coming for my head next
And no one crushed beer bottles against our walls
                          coming with marked bullets next
And the world did not call for our genocide
And a man did not call for our exile
And I did not change my hijab for protection
And the world did not fear the water
And no one called us progressive as in liberal
                          as in good as in tolerable
                  as in alive
And this hijab was not a death sentence
And this skin was not a death sentence
And refugees did not mean nothing
And Muslim bodies did not mean less
        Not at first. The next 15 years left a sour taste in
                  my mouth.

we never hire
gravediggers

Choir of Kings

In the heart of Khartoum, I heard a radio tune
about a butterfly sauce;
the brand spilling into our home,
the meter chosen to make the woman sound
as fragile as the message behind the advert. She sang

the best advice my mother gave
was to use this butterfly sauce,

and I thought, *my grandma's sauce could eat*
your mama's sauce three times over
and still have room for your aunty's too.

There's nothing fire ever taught me
that my grandmother didn't already know.
The way the air would bend to make space for her.
The ground a canvas beneath her feet.
Her light unstoppable, her force complete.

Her blood-orange nails would crack the smoke
to drop the cloves in—a hidden pinch of sugar
kept us guessing.

We Never Hire Gravediggers

I've never lived in my grandma's house
but basically everyone else has—
the widowed woman and her daughter,
the homeless man by the market
the children carried in by the drought
the tailor, the tinker, the well digger
and his camel.

When the famine came, her doors flew open
the lines of people changing
the geography of our street.

Her nest of pigeons by the pear tree,
the tamarind out back. All her things
gave of themselves so the people could eat
like kings.

She said
home is a question,
every one of us an answer.

so don't be asking questions
when you see people in my house.

I don't know what it means to not wear
my past like a fresh coat of paint
already cracked by the distance
there still is between us.

What makes a person?

Is it the things we lose, the way we crumble,
the way we fall as if each time is the first
and last time?

Is it the change we make, is it our foolishness,
our strength, the way we die, the way we come
    back
from the brink of death?
How we own everything,
but save nothing? Is it the things we pass
down from those before us?

Sometimes I wonder what
it would feel like to belong
to myself. Is it the way we break?
The way we hurt one another?

Is it our excuses, the stories we keep
and the ones we leave out? Is it other people,
the ones we keep and the ones we leave out?

Is it the steady solitude of always being
in one body no matter how much you love
another person?

We Never Hire Gravediggers

Is it the love we give and the love we don't get back?

I count my siblings every morning
to make sure they're still there.
In the back of my mind voices carry.
My own catches up. I count again.

I don't know what it means to not be me.
Sometimes I smile just to keep existing.

In her last days my grandmother carried
hot coals from her clay fire
away to a pit until the pot cooled,
halving the coals until the bubbles slowed
to a simmer the chunks to a smolder
the embers to ash,

as if she were replicating her entire life
in those moments.

and when she died, the birds migrated
from her pear tree to her bedside and back
the radio humming in her old room.
Her collection of strangers finding refuge in her house,
a procession of misfits.
A choir of kings.

Tarzan

It's kind of funny that Tarzan was a white man.
To just show up somewhere and call it his.
It's kind of funny that Disney has a movie about Africa
with no black people in it.
Just a white man and Africa.

It's kind of funny that Jane and Tarzan got together.
Jungle fever without any of the risk.
But that was back then, right?
Disney recently proposed the
Princess of North Sudan movie
in which the first African princess is played by
a white person.

In which a thousand Sudanese queens have their crowns
usurped by a girl with skin as pale as false gold
whose father had the audacity to believe
that he could just show up somewhere and call it his.
White man plants a flag in North Africa
is lauded as an excellent father for raping the motherland.

My bloodline is older than your idiocy yet here we are.
I called Disney and asked if they ever considered making
Tarzan a black man.
Turns out they did. But they only got three-fifths of the
way through the movie before they fixed it.

I've watched them tear apart our land,
take our crowns, leave our brothers bleeding on the floor
And now for $12.99 I can see it in theaters
everywhere.

The Colors We Ascribe

Our ancestors built our bodies from soil
in the creases of their hands.
We were loyal, not to the men in our lives
but to the desert clay in our bones.

This is who we were: fire wrapped in faded skin,
children of grandmothers, mothers of kings
until the day our brethren fell.

When the last breath is taken, flesh turns.
The colors of life that leave the body are the
    names we ascribe to our fears; we see rainbows
    everywhere.

The irony of fire is that your eyes go last.
Long after you can no longer feel it sting,
you can still see it burn.

In death all our eyes are gray, they mimic the hues
    of smoke that dance across the sky.
There are no instructions for dealing with death.

When the militia opened fire in El Fashir, we
    saw gold stars fall from the sky, land on every
    cornerstone, until the buildings began to melt.

They poured lead from a broken chalice, silver
    kerosene, crimson flames.

Ivory when the sun hits bone at high noon.

Burgundy when blood dries, it chips, as if it's trying
    to escape back into a body.
I can never forget how much death loves my people,
    the way they fall asleep at his feet.

Burgundy blankets, burgundy pillows,
but our tears are colorless.
There is no hue to shade this pain.

Eleven days ago, two bullets crossed off two more
    faces from my family tree,
They were 14; they were studying.
The blood-soaked arithmetic pages are sitting on the
    mantel; my uncle won't throw them away.

I can't tell you what death looks like, but when he
    came, he stayed.
We held one funeral for two brothers,

the misshapen grooves of a once body bend the light
    so, their caskets were closed,
coffins made heavy by the weight of two bullets.

My brother is thirteen and he's learning to carry
  our dead. His legs buckle under the weight of his
  pedigree.
My father says, *Stand up straight*
You think this is hard?
Try carrying the living

We never hire gravediggers anymore.
Now the soil is so familiar under my hands, I've
  gathered enough to build a body,
but I'm afraid of what I'll make.

I'm afraid to write this bloodline into something
that I'll love.

This pain is encoded.
Our genes come to fruition on our skin.
This isn't burgundy it's black.

I wake up every morning wondering
when they'll come for me.
I want to spill every color from this form.

I want to leave a canvas sinking with the weight of
   my pedigree.
I want to be able to look at a sunrise and not see my
   entire family falling to pieces.

I wish this skin had come with instructions.
When the last breath is taken, flesh turns
And for the past 21 years,
I have seen rainbows everywhere.

Bullets

My father's voice yanked me awake
My brother had been shot.
I had never felt fear like that:
waiting for that first breath on the other side of the
    line at a hospital half a world away.

The thing we had been fighting for the past
    11 years had reached the capitol and burrowed
    itself into my next of kin.

I am 21 years old and I know more about death than
    about living.
My life experiences revolve around massacres and
    funerals. I know how to start revolutions, but I
    don't know how to lose myself.

I don't know how to give in to this thing called
    youth because I know how it ends.

I called my brother an idiot and he said, *live free or
    die.* He said, *freedom is a question of life;*

if you do not reach for it, then you are not alive.

This distinct flavor of anarchy
stinks of murder, stains
like the blood of a good patriot,
and leaves a bitter thirst in your mouth
only quenched by liberation.

That week, burning cities made me feel numb,
   bullets made me think of my brother,
so I closed my eyes and prayed.
I dreamt of lead, of gutted windowpanes, of
   Damascus, of Gaza, of Baltimore
and when I awoke,

breathing made me feel guilty—
makes me feel guilty like
I should have been there,
like I should have fought,
should have stood and faced the firing squad.

When you fight for freedom, you stomach pain like
   that.

This body should be lined with bullets:
one for each of my brothers and sisters who stopped
   a *bullet* for me.

This is the mark of my generation.
We are more accustomed to the weight of Molotov
   cocktails on our bodies than we are to the embrace
   of one another.
Live free or die?
Die free or live.

I want to live in a time where civil disobedience
    doesn't end in death,
where children aren't born under the full moon of
    revolution.

Where I haven't lost more people than there are
    years in my life
I don't want this kind of wisdom.
I'm still too young for this kind of pain.

This changes you.
Not in an earth-moving, groundbreaking kind of
    way but bit by bit and with incredible stillness.
It's the little things.

Like how I cringe at the word *protest*

Like how I don't trust anyone who isn't fighting

Like how I'm as comfortable with sleeping bodies as
    I am with dead ones because it's all the same.
My brother hears me frowning through the phone
He says *smile; you'll live longer.*

For Muhannad, Taha, and Adam

I walk into the morgue
The mortician presents my country splayed across a
    table
Asks me to identify the body
I do not recognize it
Its emaciated form dimmed by a death I did not
    prepare for
I did not expect losing my culture to feel like this

This cadaver I dared to call an identity
Once held a belief that I could hold home
On the tip of my tongue,
In the breadth of my appetite
In the weight of my memories
I only recognize my country in photographs, in tour
    books
Not in living color
Not in this state of surrender

My stomach failed me first gripping down on
    processed food
The bite of bile on my disobedient tongue
My ears followed, forgetting the timbre of my
    grandfather's voice;
the swift hush of wind on desert sand

Then my accent, as they force-fed me this borrowed
    language

There's something about the taste of assimilation
    that makes you want to get back on the boat
I think of home every time the bank asks me if I
    want to go paperless
Don't they know that people of color have
    been doing that since Plymouth Rock, since
    Underground Railroad, since my uncles, turning
    my house into a refugee camp?
Red white blue, like stand your ground, like shoot to
    kill, like hate crimes
Only stars I see are when the cops roll in to take my
    neighborhood, my family, undocumented
Only stripes I see chain us to the prisons of this
    existence
I find myself talking to people across borders
more each day
I find myself crying for their countries too
This massacre
This wilted flower field of discarded nations less
    melting pot, more guillotine more disemboweled
    American dream
If you hate it so much, then why are you here?
*Because sometimes, the city collapses, and the rubble
    keeps bleeding*
*Sometimes, your blood is the only thing you can carry
    with you,*
*Sometimes, the water is more inviting than where you
    stand*

That's how you end up with little kids washed up on
foreign soil
And I'm not just talking about the ones who make it
Do you know what it's like to escape genocide only
to be gunned down in your own home?
Don't they know that they're just finishing the work
our dictator started?
Ever since they gave me the death certificate, no the
certificate of naturalization
I've been seeing ghosts, mostly in the mirror, at the
dinner table, at the family picnic
Trying to preserve culture, naive enough to believe
that we can hold home and here without anyone
having to leave

I met the president
Sat with him at a table too small to hold everything
that brought us there
His hands resting
Where are your chains? They told me your hands
were tied
When they sent those kids back, when they
wouldn't take the refugees, when they closed off
the borders but not Guantanamo
Mr. President, why do they call it the land of the
free when even the dead can't leave?
Mr. President, what does one caged bird say to
another?

But I could barely hear him over the corpse lying
    between us
He looked at me as if he thought I was afraid
Doesn't he know, that back home, the women take
    care
of the bodies?

He Left Poetry in the Spaces between My Teeth

I open my eyes to darkness so profound
it speaks, but only in parable.
My arms weigh heavy on a mattress
so cold, I feel I am not here. My window
creaks, exchanging pleasantries with the wind,
or maybe fighting. God was here. The sun set
in my head and I broke my fast with the Creator.
 My fear of all the outside things
like war, and love, and anger—

seven-stage meal, artisan buffet of grief—
lay out on the table. God is a hearty eater.
His appetite carried mine
then carried me. And we ate. We are still eating.
 Every day I am here we feast and he lets me hear
 his poetry.
He says,
Time is an expert chef, and your hunger,
I gave that to you so eat, child.
You were never meant to be wasteful.
With every difficulty, there is ease, and this ritual is
 mine.

Mama

I was walking down the street when a man stopped
   me
and said,
Hey yo sistah, you from the motherland?
Because my skin is a shade too deep not to have come
   from foreign soil
Because this garment on my head screams Africa
Because my body is a beacon calling everybody to
   come flock to the motherland
I said, *I'm Sudanese, why?*
He says, *'cause you got a little bit of flavor in you,*
I'm just admiring what your mama gave you

Let me tell you something about my mama
She can reduce a man to tattered flesh
without so much as blinking
Her words fester beneath your skin and the whole
   time,
You won't be able to stop cradling her eyes.
My mama is a woman, flawless and formidable in the
   same step.

Woman walks into a war zone and has warriors
cowering at her feet
My mama carries all of us in her body,
on her face, in her blood
And blood is no good once you let it loose
So she always holds us close.

When I was 7, my mama cradled bullets in the billows
   of her robes.
That same night, she taught me how to get gunpowder
   out of cotton with a bar of soap.
Years later when the soldiers held her at gunpoint
and asked her who she was
She said, *I am a daughter of Adam, I am a woman, who
   the hell are you?*

The last time we went home, we watched our village
   burn,
Soldiers pouring blood from civilian skulls
As if they too could turn water into wine.
They stole the ground beneath our feet.

The woman who raised me
turned and said, *don't be scared*
I'm your mother, I'm here, I won't let them through.
My mama gave me conviction.
Women like her
Inherit tired eyes,
Bruised wrists and titanium-plated spines.
The daughters of widows wearing the wings of
   amputees
Carry countries between their shoulder blades.

I'm not saying dating is a first-world problem, but
    these trifling motherfuckers seem to be.
The kind who'll quote Rumi, but not know what he
    sacrificed for war.
Who'll fawn over Lupita, but turn their racial filters
    on.
Who'll take their politics with a latte when I take
    mine with tear gas.
Every guy I meet wants to be my introduction to the
    dark side,
Wants me to open up this obsidian skin and let them
    read every tearful page,
Because what survivor hasn't had her struggle made
    spectacle?

Don't talk about the motherland unless you know
that being from Africa means waking up an
    afterthought
in this country.
Don't talk about my flavor unless you know
that my flavor is insurrection, it is rebellion,
    resistance
My flavor is mutiny
It is burden, it is grit, and it is compromise
And you don't know compromise until you've
    rebuilt your home for the third time
Without bricks, without mortar, without any other
    option

I turned to the man and said,
My mother and I can't walk the streets alone
back home anymore.
Back home, there are no streets to walk anymore.

My Sudan

My parents named me "Emtithal"
Image of perfection, God's will come to fruition

The first gift my parents gave me was a promise,
an age-old epic of home of home,
of warriors past and new—

the craftsmen, the artists, the teachers, the doctors,
the mostly doctors—

the place where queens and beggars eat
at the same dinner table and call it family.

This is history we grew up on, a heat-packed
  journey
through the Sahara and into the forest.

My Sudan is green, and red, and an azure
like a sky so blue your mouth would water
when the clouds passed by.

It is silver, like the coins my grandpa tied in his belt
And bronze, like the brick-maker's hands.

We Never Hire Gravediggers

The Sudan I knew sings loud and laughs even
   louder.
Its face is warm, a smile, like the strangers who
   fought for you
before you were born.

She carries a walking stick and a baby's bottle,
an ice pick for the popsicles in the market and
a woven basket for the summer's grain.

My Sudan is quick, quicker than the birds that
steal the guava fruit, and lean,
leaner than the date palm tree—
toolik tool al ban wa aglik agl al daan—
my Sudan has jokes, like my father likes to say:
you are as tall as a palm tree and as dumb as a goat

because he knows he made me smart,
and we make them smart:

we make the people who brave the water when the
   tide is high
who conjure medicine when the hour is nigh
the people who build clocks, even though we're
   always late

my Sudan has hope like the parents who rebuild
without a promise of tomorrow
or the kids who bring an umbrella even if it hasn't
    rained
in decades

My Sudan is beautiful, and when my homeland cries
everyone listens, no, everyone weeps
because we are one body, one land in two countries,
one love in the hearts of many, one family
in the homes of many

We're the generation with a world-class team of
    engineers, lawyers, lab techs, and chefs, teachers
    and entrepreneurs,
to call *mom* and *dad, aunty* and *uncle*

In my sanctuary I think of home, of the faces that
    watched us grow. This is our legacy, memories of
    sesame candy
And mouthy neighbors, and weddings so loud
they'd call the cops on us every time

and summers full attending graduations
with enough degrees to pave any wall
enough outfits to call the lunch table the silk road

these days our warriors have turned to worriers,
our castles into sidewalk heavens, but we're still
that place, that fresh fruit taste,
that promise.

I'm proud to be part of that promise kept.

Eulogy

Black girl writes eulogy in the flesh.
They took my skin;
Paraded it around the town square;
pinned their desire, their hatred to it;
Hung it on their clotheslines;
Fastened it over the eyes of their children
so they wouldn't see me.

Blanket. Burial shroud. Body.
My mother gave birth to me in a casket.
I never grew out of it.

I had a dream last night: they strung me up
like a psalm, but this time,
The noose said, *no.*

The poplar tree leapt from her place
and carried me to my mother.
Spoiled fruit to an unknowing owner.
She couldn't see me. They had taken her eyes,
Her mouth, her feet.

Run. Run, run, run, run, run.
I've been stuck here for so long
and no one came.
300 of my sisters disappeared
and no one came.

Black girl dies no one knows.
Black girl funeral is an empty house.
The spectacle of my body is an empty threat.
Black girl don't make headlines,
Build no search parties.

They dragged my body out of the river
but it was the wrong girl.

index

Afternoon Naps in the House of God   14

August   9

Bird-Watching on Lesvos Island   62

Boy in the Sand   53

Bullets   100

Choir of Kings   90

Cinderblock   44

Classrooms   50

Dad   76

Deliverance in the Information Age   71

Dr. Poem   58

Eulogy   116

Euphoria at Community Prayer   16

Index

For Muhannad, Taha, and Adam   103

Head over Heels   54

He Left Poetry in the Spaces between My Teeth   107

How to Translate a Joke   37

Islamophobia   86

Jezebel   31

Loose Threads   15

Mama   108

Millennial   80

#MuslimParents   17

My Sudan   112

No Funeral   45

No One Says How Easy It Is to Fall in Love,
   or How Hard It Is to Stay There   81

October, or My Uncle Calls to Say
   Grandma Has Died   75

One-Drop Well   19

People Like Us   2

Prospects   35

September   46

Sesame Candy   13

She Threw Things out of Windows
    and I Watched   47

Sisters' Entrance   10

Sustenance   23

Take Notes   68

Tarzan   94

Telephone   36

Tenets   70

The Bride   25

The Colors We Ascribe   96

The Imam on Charity   18

The Talk   22

The Things She Told Me   29

To Envy a Scavenger   69

Tower Two   87

Why I Haven't Told You Yet   32

Year-Round   24

You Have a Big Imagination, or
    400,000 Ways to Cry   72

Andrews McMeel Publishing
a division of Andrews McMeel Universal
1130 Walnut Street, Kansas City, Missouri 64106

www.andrewsmcmeel.com

18 19 20 21 22 BVG 10 9 8 7 6 5 4 3 2 1

ISBN: 978-1-4494-9279-3

Library of Congress Control Number: 2018936781

Editor: Patty Rice
Art Director: Diane Marsh
Production Editor: David Shaw
Production Manager: Cliff Koehler
Cover Art: Emtithal Mahmoud

Attention: Schools and Businesses

Andrews McMeel books are available at
quantity discounts with bulk purchase for
educational, business, or sales promotional use.
For information, please e-mail the Andrews
McMeel Publishing Special Sales Department:
specialsales@amuniversal.com.